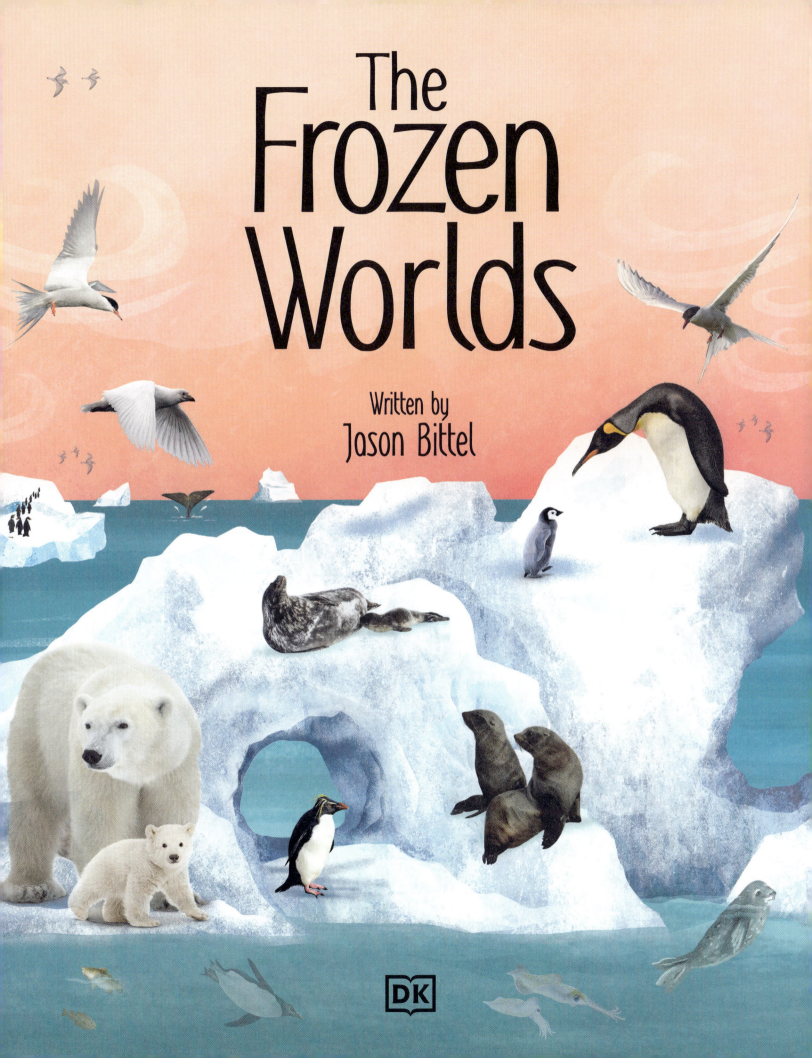

The Frozen Worlds

Written by
Jason Bittel

DK

DK | Penguin Random House

Author Jason Bittel
Illustrator Claire McElfatrick
Consultant Simon Morley
Project Editor Sophie Parkes
Senior Art Editor Claire Patane
Editor Sarah MacLeod
Designers Polly Appleton, Eleanor Bates, Hannah Moore
Picture Researcher Sakshi Saluja
Senior Production Editor Dragana Puvacic
Senior Production Controller Inderjit Bhullar
Jacket Designer Claire Patane
Jacket Editor Issy Walsh
Managing Editor Penny Smith
Deputy Art Editor Mabel Chan
Publishing Director Sarah Larter

First published in Great Britain in 2023 by
Dorling Kindersley Limited
DK, One Embassy Gardens, 8 Viaduct Gardens,
London, SW11 7BW

The authorised representative in the EEA is
Dorling Kindersley Verlag GmbH. Arnulfstr. 124,
80636 Munich, Germany

Copyright © 2023 Dorling Kindersley Limited
A Penguin Random House Company
10 9 8 7 6 5 4 3 2
004–332939–Mar/2023

A CIP catalogue record for this book
is available from the British Library.
ISBN: 978-0-2415-8507-8

Printed and bound in China

For the curious
www.dk.com

INTRODUCTION

When people think about the Arctic
and Antarctic, they tend to picture
ice. And while there's certainly a lot
of that, there's also an unbelievable
amount of life!

From clever orcas and super-fast
penguins, to globe-trotting terns
and 400-year-old sharks, Earth's
coldest and harshest environments
support many creatures and hold
many surprises! In summer, the
Arctic explodes with colourful
flowers. In Antartica, scientists live
year-round in special laboratories
that look like space stations.

Join me on an incredible adventure
through the frozen worlds.

Jason Bittel

CONTENTS

Most of icebergs lie beneath the water's surface.

WHAT IS THE ARCTIC AND ANTARCTIC?

These amazing snowy, icy places are found on opposite sides of the Earth – the Arctic far in the north, and the Antarctic in the far south.

Particular animals can be found at one pole or the other, but never both. **Penguins** are found in the southern part of the world and Antarctica, while **polar bears** only live in the Arctic.

Icebergs, glaciers, and ice volcanoes, make the frozen worlds some of the most hostile places on Earth, but as you will see, they are also places of **awesome beauty and wonder**.

Pacific Ocean

THE ARCTIC

The Arctic is an ocean surrounded by continents. It covers a large area, also known as the Arctic Circle, with Earth's **North Pole** at its centre. It includes a huge expanse of solid ice and the northern tips of **Asia**, **Europe**, and **North America**.

Arctic tern

North America

Asia

Reindeer

Arctic Ocean

Arctic wolf

The North Pole
This is Earth's most northern point.

Arctic fox

Musk ox

Arctic hare

Polar bears

Norwegian Sea

Europe

Inuit fishing

Narwhal

Arctic tern

Arctic sea ice can be up to 4 m (13 ft) thick.

The Arctic

LIFE IN THE ARCTIC
Arctic animals need to be able to survive in freezing conditions. To keep them warm, they have thick layers of feathers, fur, or fat.

Antarctica is the coldest and driest place on Earth. It has so little rain that it is classed as a desert.

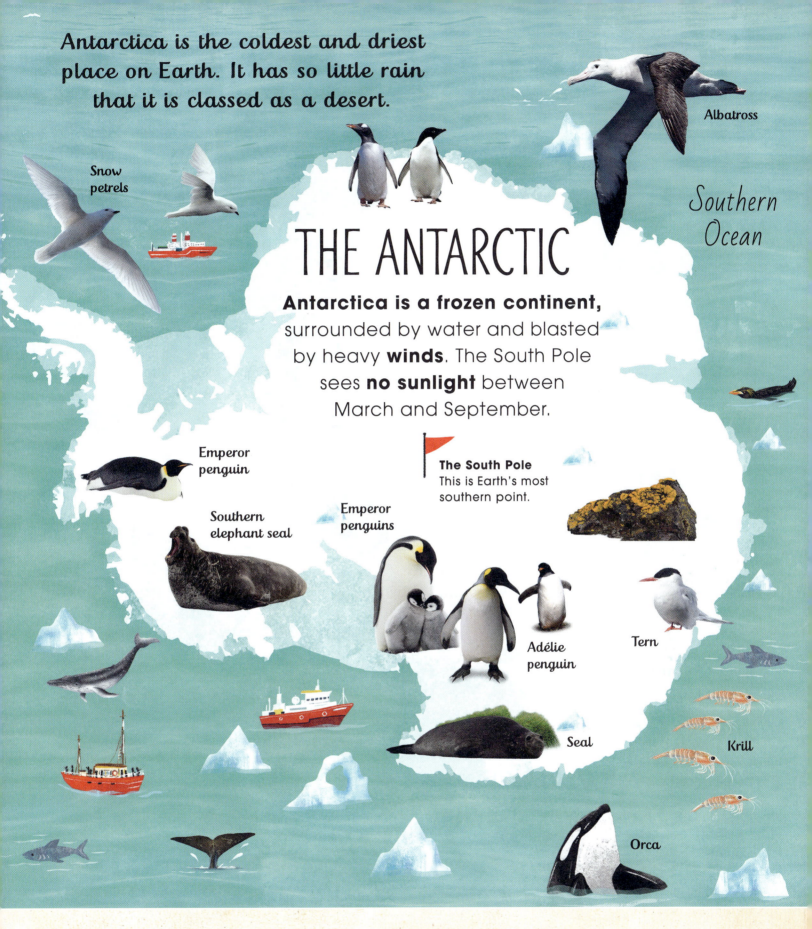

Albatross

Snow petrels

Southern Ocean

THE ANTARCTIC

Antarctica is a frozen continent, surrounded by water and blasted by heavy **winds**. The South Pole sees **no sunlight** between March and September.

Emperor penguin

Southern elephant seal

Emperor penguins

The South Pole
This is Earth's most southern point.

Adélie penguin

Tern

Seal

Krill

Orca

LIFE IN THE ANTARCTIC

Antarctic conditions are harsh, but some animals do live here. Most of them are birds and seals – there are no large land animals.

The Antarctic

Ice survivors

Survival is an everyday battle for creatures that make the poles their home. Antarctica has the lowest recorded temperatures on the planet, while the Arctic is an ever-changing maze of ice, snow, and frigid seas.

STAYING WARM

Many polar animals are larger than their cousins that live in warmer places, which means they lose less heat. But they have many ways of beating the chill.

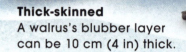

Thick-skinned
A walrus's blubber layer can be 10 cm (4 in) thick.

Arctic fox

Fur
An Arctic fox's thick, dense fur helps it to keep a warm body temperature of 40°C (104°F).

King penguin

Arctic tern

Feathery layers
Fluffy, downy penguin feathers are protected by a stiff outer layer of feathers.

Moulting
King penguins stay waterproof by replacing their worn-out feathers each year.

Feathers
Penguins stay toasty and dry thanks to short, overlapping layers of waterproof feathers.

To survive the extreme cold, polar animals have evolved unique bodies and behaviours.

Walrus

Blubber layer
This fatty tissue covers the walrus' entire body to keep it warm.

Blubber
Marine mammals are protected from the cold by a thick layer of fat, called blubber, beneath their skin.

Polar bear

Powerful paws
Polar bears have huge, snowshoe-like feet that help them push their bodies through the icy waters.

Tobogganing
Gentoo penguins take to their bellies to scoot across the snow and ice, using their flippers to guide them.

Gentoo penguins

MOVING AROUND
Polar animals are perfectly adapted to the challenge of roaming ice, snow, and freezing water.

Camouflage

In the Arctic, the landscape is white and snowy in the winter, and brown and green in the summer. To help them blend in, some of the animals that live here change colour. As the weather gets colder, they swap their brown fur or feathers for pristine white winter coats.

Top tips
Ears have black tips and insides.

Red eye
The male ptarmigan has a splash of red above its eye.

Fluffy feet
Feathers on the legs and feet help to keep the bird warm.

ROCK PTARMIGAN

This bird spends most of its life on the ground. Its feathers change to provide camouflage through the seasons – they are white in winter and brown in the summer.

ARCTIC HARE

This hare is bright white in the winter and brown or grey in the summer. Its white winter coat makes it hard for predators to spot against the snow.

The hairs of the Arctic fox's winter coat are much thicker than those of its summer coat.

Scarf or tail?
The fox can wrap itself in its long, fluffy tail, to keep it warm.

Soft as silk
The weasel's winter fur is soft and silky.

LEAST WEASEL

Arctic days are shorter in the winter than in the summer. The shortening days tell the least weasel to begin growing white hairs instead of brown.

ARCTIC FOX

Most Arctic foxes are grey or black in the summer and pure white in the winter. Their sharp hearing helps them uncover tiny prey animals hiding under the snow.

Summer

Breeding season
Many species of polar birds mate and breed during summer.

Gyrfalcon

As Earth orbits the Sun over the year, the hemisphere (half) that tilts towards the Sun experiences summer. This season is most extreme at the Earth's poles.

Ross's goose

During polar summers, the Sun never fully sets.

"Land of the Midnight Sun"
Norway is nicknamed this because more than half its area lies inside the Arctic Circle, leading to extra long days in summer.

Hot and buggy
Biting insects swarm in the summer, causing reindeer to have to move constantly to escape them.

Reindeer

Reindeer on the move
Also known as caribou, reindeer can migrate up to 640 km (400 miles) during the Arctic summer to get to their calving grounds, where they give birth to their young.

Reindeer

NORTH AND SOUTH POLES

Seasons at the North and South Poles are opposite.
This is because when one pole tilts towards the Sun and experiences summer, the other tilts away from the Sun and experiences winter.

Winter

Winter is the season that happens when one of Earth's hemispheres is tilted away from the Sun. At the poles, this means plants and animals must endure darkness for months on end.

During polar winters, the Sun never fully rises.

Six months of darkness
Imagine a night that lasts half a year and you'll have a good idea of what it's like to live at the poles in winter.

Life in the north
About 4 million people live in the Arctic.

Ivory gull

Polar bears

Winter babies
Arctic polar bears usually give birth in December, when their world is dark.

Winter is a time of plenty for animals such as polar bears, and summer can be a time of hunger.

Icebergs

An iceberg is a chunk of freshwater ice that is more than 15 m (50 ft) long. Icebergs form when a section of ice breaks away from a glacier or an ice shelf. The new iceberg then floats freely in the ocean. Some icebergs are as small as cars, and others are as big as small countries!

Pointed top

Flat top

Uneven sides

Steep, near-vertical sides

ICE ISLAND

This towering chunk of ice is an iceberg that has broken off from the edge of an ice shelf. Ice islands are also known as "tabular" icebergs. They are square-ish in shape and can be very large.

NON-TABULAR

Not all icebergs have flat tops and sides. More irregular icebergs are called "non-tabular" icebergs. They come in a wide range of different shapes and sizes.

FLAT-TOPPED

These icebergs have short sides and a smooth, flat top. Some of them are perfectly rectangular.

DOMED

The sides of these icebergs rise up steadily, creating a smooth, round dome shape.

PINNACLED

These icebergs have at least one tall column rising up from their base.

SLOPING

These icebergs are formed when tabular icebergs tilt. They have straight sides and a sloping top.

Only 10 per cent of an iceberg sticks up above the water, where we can see it. Most of its bulk is hidden beneath the waves.

DRY-DOCKED

Weather and waves wear away at icebergs. This can create a "dry-docked" shape, with a U-shaped hole.

BLOCKY

Tall and imposing, these icebergs are shaped like enormous boxes. They have very straight, steep sides.

WEATHERED

Over time, parts of icebergs can be worn away. Some of them develop arches right through the middle.

WEDGE

These are tabular icebergs that have tilted. They have trianglular sides, which narrow up to a point at the top.

Brinicles

When seawater freezes, salt is forced out of the crystals, which creates very cold, very salty liquid called brine. When the brine trickles down to the ocean floor, it causes the water around it to freeze instantly, creating a hollow icicle known as a brinicle.

Brinicle

Jellyfish

Cold killer

The brinicle grows slowly down through the water. When it reaches the seafloor, it hardens into an icy path, freezing and killing any creature that is unfortunate enough to get in its way.

The brinicle's icy path

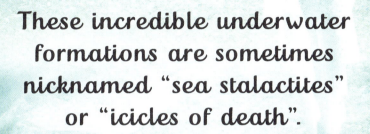

These incredible underwater
formations are sometimes
nicknamed "sea stalactites"
or "icicles of death".

Seals

Blue bloods
A blue, copper-based protein
helps octopus blood to carry
oxygen in the cold. It also
makes their blood look blue!

**Antarctic
octopus**

Air-breathers
Some animals, such as seals,
hunt beneath the ice, but
need to swim up to the
water's surface to breathe.

**Antarctic
notothenioid
fish**

Benthos
Seafloor creatures, known
as benthos, survive by eating
food that falls from above,
and each other!

Sea star

Old and cold
Benthos grow slowly,
but can live for
many decades.

**Sea
urchin**

Fire and ice

Despite being covered in ice, the Arctic and Antarctic are also home to volcanoes. West Antarctica has more than 130 volcanoes, and there are probably many more waiting to be discovered. In fact, these ice-covered volcanoes make up the largest volcanic region on Earth!

Scientists discovered **91 new volcanoes...**

Lava

MOUNT EREBUS

Mount Erebus in Antarctica is the southernmost active volcano on Earth. Unlike many other volcanoes, it has a lake of lava in its central crater all year round.

Lava lakes
Only eight volcanoes in the world have bubbling lakes of lava like Mount Erebus.

Underground and underwater

Most of Antarctica's volcanoes are buried and hidden under an ice sheet 3 km (1.8 miles) thick. It also has volcanoes under the water, such as Deception Island – an active volcano that sits mostly underwater.

Ice caves
Hot steam from Mount Erebus has hollowed out areas of ice around the volcano to form ice caves.

Only a handful of the volcanoes hidden below Antarctica's massive sheet of ice are thought to be active.

...beneath the West Antarctic Ice Sheet in 2017.

Icy dangers

Scientists have only recently discovered many of these volcanoes. They don't yet know what will happen when these volcanoes erupt, but it is possible that underground volcanoes in Antarctica could melt some of the ice if they do.

BEERENBERG

Glacier-covered Beerenberg is the northernmost active volcano on Earth's surface. It is located on an island called Jan Mayen, which is in the Arctic area of Norway. It last erupted in 1985.

Bear Mountain
Beerenberg is Dutch for "Bear Mountain". It is named after the polar bears seen there by whalers in the 1600s.

Polar bear

Rare bears
The possibility of sighting a polar bear on Beerenberg is now considered very low.

Rivers through ice

With liquid rivers, lakes, and giant waterfalls, the Earth's poles aren't just ice. Some rivers form when snow is blown away, revealing dark ice beneath. This ice absorbs sunlight and warms up, causing more snow and ice to melt.

The Earth's poles aren't completely frozen!

River

ANTARCTICA

During summer in Antarctica, when more ice melts, around 700 rivers and smaller streams form across the continent, carrying melted ice back to the sea.

Scientists are still trying to learn how polar

Ponds

As polar ice melts, it can collect to form ponds. Fed by streams, some of these ponds can reach 80 km (50 miles) long!

Melt pond

Rivers under the ice

Huge rivers transport water between lakes 500 m (1,640 ft) beneath the surface. These rivers even house amphipods – tiny relatives of crabs.

Glaciers

Not quite rivers, glaciers can be found across the polar regions. They are massive bodies of ice that move very slowly across land.

Waterfalls

Where meltwater rivers meet the edge of the ice shelf, beautiful, icy-blue waterfalls form.

Waterfall

ARCTIC

The Arctic has rivers, too. There are five major rivers that dump huge quantities of fresh water from North America, Europe, and Asia into the Arctic Ocean.

meltwater affects rising sea levels and climate change.

Auroras

Also known as the Northern and Southern Lights, auroras are natural light displays that can sometimes be seen at night near the Arctic and Antarctic Circles. They look like fires, curtains, or ribbons of light that shimmer and dance along the horizon.

Auroras are named after the **Roman goddess...**

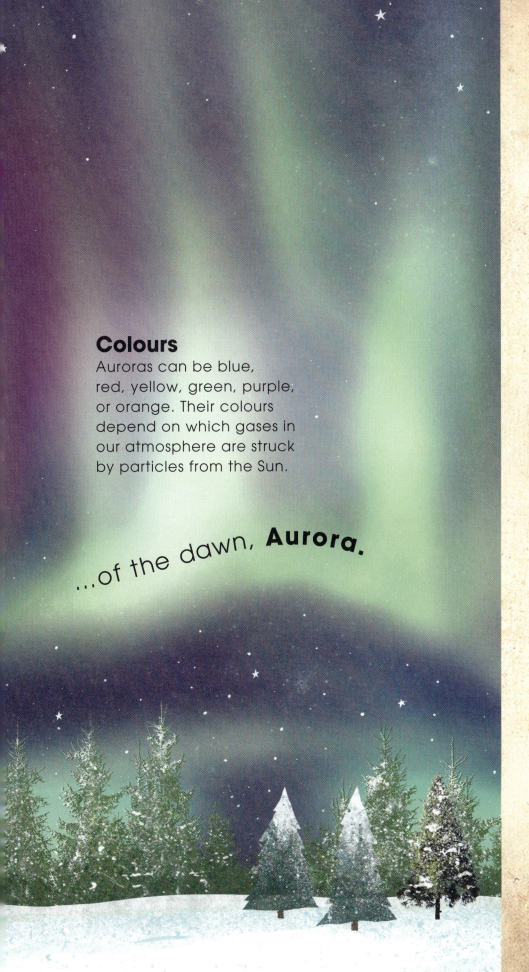

Colours

Auroras can be blue, red, yellow, green, purple, or orange. Their colours depend on which gases in our atmosphere are struck by particles from the Sun.

...of the dawn, **Aurora.**

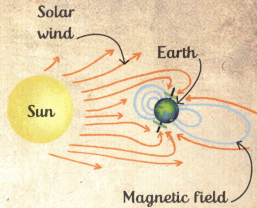

Solar wind

Sun

Earth

Magnetic field

How and why?

Particles from the Sun, carried by the solar wind, collide with gases in the Earth's atmosphere and form auroras. They usually occur at the poles because the shape of the Earth's magnetic field deflects the particles towards the poles.

Aurora Borealis

Aurora Australis

North and South

Auroras are called Aurora Borealis when they appear in the Earth's northern hemisphere, and Aurora Australis in the southern hemisphere.

This mother and baby polar bear are sheltering in the trees of Wapusk National Park in Canada.

ARCTIC LIFE

You might imagine the Arctic as a dark and empty place, but it is actually bursting with life.

Narwhals and Greenland sharks glide through the waters, while polar bears prowl on land. **Seals and walruses search for food** in the ocean and come up to land to rest or raise their young. **Millions of seabirds flock** to the area each summer. And on the shores and tundra, colourful **flowers even manage to blossom.**

Of course, there are people here too, the first of whom came to the Arctic at least 45,000 years ago!

Arctic tundra

There's more to the northern polar landscape than lifeless snow and ice. Summer's arrival sees an explosion of colour from wildflowers, shrubs, and plant-like lichens, and birds arrive by the tens of millions to breed.

Arctic skua

Musk oxen

King eiders

Wetlands
Melting snow and ice create important freshwater habitats such as bogs and fens.

Polar bear

What is tundra?
The Arctic tundra is made up of flat, rolling plains that are so far north that the winter cold prevents trees from taking root. The word tundra comes from the Finnish word *tunturi*, meaning "treeless plain".

Red-necked phalarope

Permafrost

As its name suggests, permafrost is a frozen layer of tundra soil that can occur anywhere from the Earth's surface to hundreds of feet below it. It remains frozen for most or all of the year.

Reindeer

Migration
Reindeer migrate hundreds of kilometres to the tundra each summer.

Arctic hares

Full of life

Despite low rainfall, extreme temperatures, and food shortages, hundreds of plant and animal species have found ways to survive on the tundra.

Arctic fox

Arctic mammals

Few mammals make their home in the Arctic, as it is a harsh ecosystem, but the ones that do are impressive creatures. The region is home to the two biggest species of bear in the world: the polar bear and the brown bear.

Foraging
Reindeer use their antlers to dig in snow for food.

Reindeer

Arctic hares

Cold climate
This hardy fox can survive in temperatures as low as -50°C (-58°F).

Arctic fox

Brown bear

Many Arctic mammals have beautiful white coats that help

Arctic wolves

Pack life
Wolves work together to bring down large prey such as reindeer and musk oxen.

Fur coat
A musk ox's fur is eight times warmer than a sheep's wool!

Musk oxen

NEW ARRIVALS
As the Arctic warms up due to climate change, woody plants are growing further north than ever before. Some animals, such as the ones below, are following plants north, as the region becomes more livable for them.

American beaver

Polar bear

Lemming

Ice bear
Polar bear fur looks white, but it's actually transparent (clear).

Strength not size
Wolverines are ferocious predators. They can crush bones of animals much larger than themselves.

Wolverine

Arctic engineers
Beavers eat the woody plants and also use them to build dams. These dams create ponds, which could be causing the permafrost below them to thaw, reshaping the landscape.

them blend in with the ice and snow.

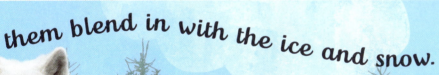

Constant coat
The Arctic wolf has white fur all year round.

European elk

CAMOUFLAGE
A white coat helps many Arctic animals blend in with their surroundings. This allows predators such as the Arctic wolf to sneak up on prey.

Giant deer
European elk, or moose, are the largest deer species. They rely on woody plants for food and prefer a cold habitat, so their numbers are booming in the Arctic where it is cooler.

Snow goose

Red-throated loon

King eider

Show-offs
King eider males have colourful faces of yellow, orange, and red.

Common loon

Tundra swan

Snowy owl

Tundra

Some birds, such as the snowy owl, nest right on the ground in the treeless plains of the tundra. The open space allows them to see in all directions so they can protect their nests.

Red phalarope

Long-tailed jaeger

Arctic birds

About 200 species of birds call the Arctic home for at least part of the year. Some travel thousands of miles (migrate) to get there, even from as far away as Antarctica. Others brave the temperatures all year round.

Tundra chickens
Rock ptarmigan are chicken-sized, ground-nesting birds related to grouse.

Male

Female

Rock ptarmigan

Common eiders

Snow
bunting

Migration

Why travel halfway across the world?
Birds that migrate to the Arctic each
summer have to worry about fewer
predators and parasites there.

Jetsetters
From Antarctica to
the Arctic Circle, Arctic
terns have the longest
migration of any animal.

Arctic tern

Peregrine
falcon

Black-legged
kittiwakes

Black
guillemots

Atlantic
puffin

Northern
gannets

Cliffs

Rocky outcrops provide safe
places for birds to breed in the
Arctic, sheltered from the cold
and away from predators.

King of gulls
The great
black-backed gull
is the largest gull
in the world.

Great black-
backed gull

White-tailed
eagle

Ruddy turnstone

Sanderling

Western
sandpiper

Deep dive
The little auk can
dive to depths
of 35 m (115 ft)
to catch fish.

Northern fulmar

Water

Many birds of the Arctic are
excellent swimmers and divers. This
includes the Atlantic puffin, which
can dive and swim underwater
to hunt fish to eat.

Razorbill

Little auk

Life in the water

From deep-diving birds to underwater unicorn horns, the creatures of the Arctic have had to evolve some curious features and behaviours to survive in the chilly world beneath the Arctic's ice.

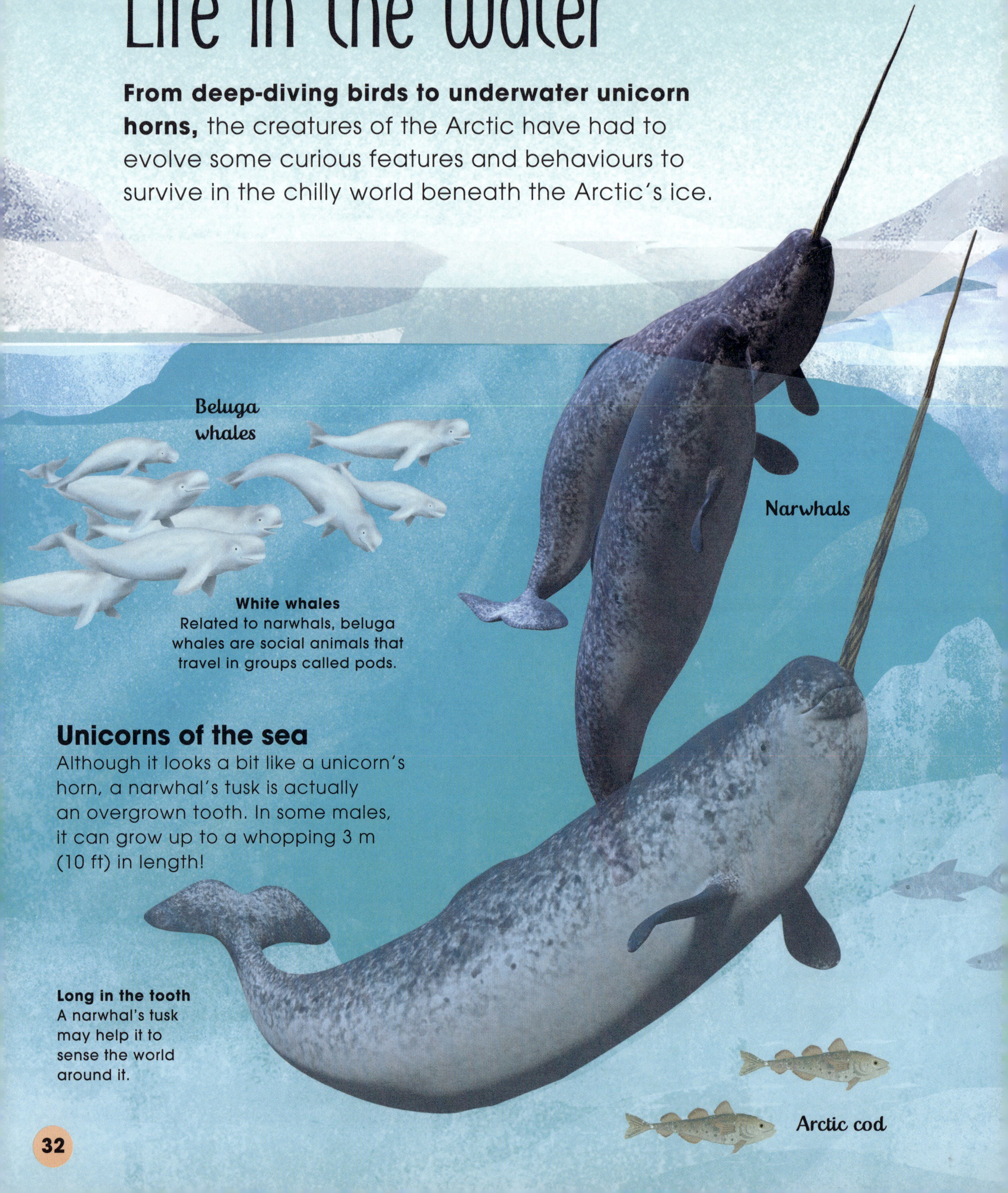

Beluga whales

White whales
Related to narwhals, beluga whales are social animals that travel in groups called pods.

Narwhals

Unicorns of the sea
Although it looks a bit like a unicorn's horn, a narwhal's tusk is actually an overgrown tooth. In some males, it can grow up to a whopping 3 m (10 ft) in length!

Long in the tooth
A narwhal's tusk may help it to sense the world around it.

Arctic cod

Walruses

Fish detectives
Super-sensitive whiskers help walruses find tasty shellfish in the ground.

Harp seals

Ice nursery
Baby harp seals are born in large groups out on the floating sea ice.

Many Arctic mammals sport a thick layer of blubber to keep them toasty in the freezing Arctic climate.

Arctic haddock

Diving birds
Guillemots can dive as deep as 180m (590 ft) underwater in search of fish.

Guillemots

Walrus

Greenland shark

They might be less well known than iconic great white sharks, but Greenland sharks are mighty record-breakers. Scientists think this huge species can live to be more than 400 years old! These ancient giants are quite mysterious to scientists, who still don't know much about them.

Greenland sharks live longer than any other vertebrates on the planet!

Cold water giants
A Greenland shark can weigh up to 1.3 tonnes (1.5 tons) and grow longer than a giraffe is tall!

Sleeper sharks
Greenland sharks are a type of sleeper shark, that are named for how they slowly sneak up on prey.

There could be a Greenland shark **alive today...**

Everything from reindeer to polar bears have been found in Greenland sharks' stomachs.

World travellers

Greenland sharks were once thought to exist only in the frigid waters of the Arctic. However, recently they have been spotted as far south as Belize in Central America. Scientists think the deep ocean may be cool enough to keep them comfortable.

Anti-freeze

Chemicals in their body tissues stop the sharks from freezing. This helps them survive some of the coldest places on Earth.

Scavengers

Greenland sharks are carnivores and scavengers. They prey upon fish, squid, and marine mammals such as seals.

Vision loss

Greenland sharks are often found with small, parasitic crustaceans growing on their eyeballs. This can cause the sharks to become partially blind, but does not seem to bother them.

...that was also living **in the 1600s!**

Trees

The Arctic tundra tends to lack trees. However, as climate change raises temperatures, certain types of trees, such as spruce, have started to grow further north.

Arctic plants

While much of the Arctic is open sea and ice, about 1,700 kinds of plants take root in the most northern parts of Europe, Asia, and North America. They must survive harsh winters, but summers of near-constant sunlight help the plants to thrive.

Arctic willow

Built for winter

To prevent them from freezing solid, Arctic plants have special adaptations. They often have short root systems and grow low to the ground.

Arctic poppy

Boreal pixie-cup lichen

Common freckle pelt lichen

Sphagnum moss

Lichens

They look like plants, but lichens are actually living things made of a combination of fungus and algae. They can grow almost anywhere, and provide food, homes, and nesting material for animals.

Reindeer cup lichen

Bearberry

Fireweed

Flowers

In summer, the Arctic
explodes with colour.
Some flowers last just a
few days, but each one
is an important source of
nutrition for Arctic wildlife.

Cotton
grass

Yellow marsh
saxifrage

Mouse-eared
chickweed

Purple
saxifrage

Sphagnum moss

Polytrichum
moss

Mosses

Carpet-like mosses grow where other
plants cannot. They draw moisture from
the air and soil, but can also survive
periods of drought and extreme cold.

Arctic arthropods

No ecosystem would be complete without bugs, and the Arctic is no exception! From pollinators to parasites, tons of insects and arachnids have found some surprising ways to thrive and survive in the harsh, chilly north.

Arctic bumblebee

Arctic woolly bear moth

Anti-freeze
Chemicals in this caterpillar's blood protect it when it freezes solid!

Arctic woolly bear moth caterpillar

Flower power
Cone-shaped flowers funnel the Sun's warmth, helping the bees warm up.

Arctic woolly bear moth
Most caterpillars transform into moths and butterflies in their first year, but not the Arctic woolly bear moth. The Arctic chill forces the moth to take its time. It can live seven years before changing into a moth, a process called metamorphosis.

Arctic bumblebee
Bumblebees can't fly when they're cold. They sunbathe to warm themselves, as well as "shivering" their large flight muscles to create heat. Thick fur and a slightly larger-than-normal size also help these insects stay comfy in the cold.

Bloodsuckers
Female mosquitos drink animal blood to obtain protein, which they use to grow eggs.

Mosquito

Tiny terrors
Miniscule midges are so small that they're also known as "no-see-ums".

Midge

Tick

Hitchhiking ticks
Ticks perch on grass and lie in wait for a meal to wander by.

Blood feeders

Many parasites have made a home in the Arctic, where they drink the nutritious blood of larger animals to survive. High numbers of these tiny creatures can force the movement of larger animals, such as reindeer.

Circle of life
Once the larvae are sneezed out of a reindeer's nose and onto the ground, they mature into adults to repeat the bizarre cycle.

Reindeer

Larva

Safe and sound
More than 50 botfly larvae can occupy just one reindeer's nasal cavity. The warmth of the nose and throat help the larvae survive winter.

Adult botfly

Botfly

Reindeer are key to the survival of botflies. The parasitic flies lay their larvae on a reindeer's face, where the young are able to wriggle into the reindeer's nostrils and throat for winter. In spring, the larvae let go and the reindeer sneezes them out.

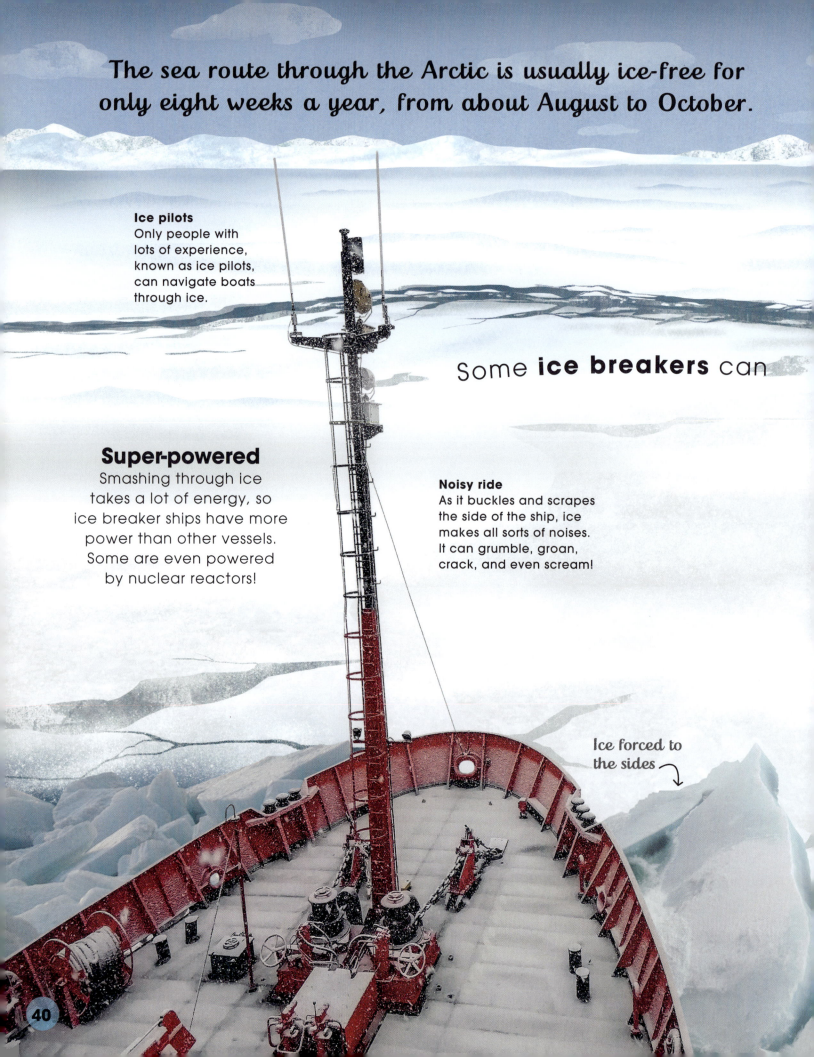

The sea route through the Arctic is usually ice-free for only eight weeks a year, from about August to October.

Ice pilots
Only people with lots of experience, known as ice pilots, can navigate boats through ice.

Some **ice breakers** can

Super-powered
Smashing through ice takes a lot of energy, so ice breaker ships have more power than other vessels. Some are even powered by nuclear reactors!

Noisy ride
As it buckles and scrapes the side of the ship, ice makes all sorts of noises. It can grumble, groan, crack, and even scream!

Ice forced to the sides ↘

Ships rely on ice breakers to lead the way through the Arctic ice for the rest of the year.

Normal ship

Buddy system
Normal ships hire ice breakers to carve paths through the ice in front of them. They follow closely behind.

travel through ice 5 m (16 ft) thick.

Ice breaker

Breaking the ice
Ice breakers have very strong hulls (bodies), to help them withstand the force of slamming into the ice. Curved bows (fronts) allow them to slide on top of thick ice, so it cracks under the ship's weight.

Wide load
A special shape – wide at the front and narrower at the back – allows an ice breaker to clear a path through the thick ice for other ships.

Ice breakers

One of the easiest and most direct ways for ships to cross the northern hemisphere is through the Arctic Circle. But there's one problem: ice, and lots of it! The solution? Huge, strong ice breaker ships specially built to carve pathways through the thick layer of frozen water.

Life in the Arctic

Indigenous peoples have been in the Arctic for at least 45,000 years. There are more than 40 different ethnic groups, from Saami in northern Europe, to Nenets and Khanty in Russia, to Aleut and Yupik in Alaska. Both Indigenous and non-indigenous peoples live there still, but life is different now.

Shaky ground
Climate change is causing permafrost to melt. This threatens to topple the buildings and roads that have been built on top of it. The melting could also disrupt water supplies.

Catch of the day
People mostly rely on foods they catch, such as fish, seals, and reindeer. Fruits, vegetables, and foods such as biscuits and fizzy drinks have to be brought in by boat (but only when the ice has melted enough) or by plane. This makes them very expensive.

Fishing

Snowmobiles

Light aircraft

Getting around

Some Arctic communities have airstrips so that small planes can transport people and goods. For thousands of years, people used sleds pulled by dogs to travel across the snow. Nowadays, they are more likely to use snowmobiles.

On the move

Some people have a nomadic lifestyle. This means they are always moving to follow the reindeer herds as the seasons change.

Reindeer

People have found many ways to survive in some of the most remote places on Earth.

At home and out hunting

Buildings such as these colourful, wood-panelled houses in Greenland are common in the Arctic. Inuit, an indigenous group widespread across the Arctic, use igloos for shelters on hunting and fishing trips, as well as for cultural ceremonies.

Ice roads

In winter, ice roads are built over frozen tundra, lakes, and rivers.

Dressing for the weather

Traditionally, people living in the Arctic would have made clothes from the skins and furs of animals they hunted, such as seals or bears. Today, they are more likely to wear machine-made materials.

Life in Arctic cities

Cities in the Arctic? Yes, they do exist! In fact, there are 10 cities north of the Arctic Circle with populations of 30,000 people or more. The largest is Murmansk in Russia.

Harsh habitats

Some cities, such as Norilsk in Russia, can only be reached by boat or plane, as they don't have roads in or out! The temperatures can be a challenge too. Murmansk in winter can drop as low as -39.4°C (-38.9°F).

Long days and nights

Most of these cities have at least one day every winter when the Sun doesn't rise, and at least one day every summer when the Sun doesn't set.

Treeless cities
Because they are so far north, most Arctic cities don't have any trees.

Arctic activities

There are lots of good things about living in the Arctic. The long nights can bring beautiful sunsets and auroras. People enjoy snowsports such as skiing and hiking.

Arctic communities
Both Indigenous and non-indigenous people inhabit the Arctic cities.

Arctic exploration

Starting in the early 1800s, explorers became obsessed with trying to become the first outsiders to travel to the North Pole. Two teams claimed to have accomplished the feat on separate expeditions in 1908 and 1909, but experts can't say for sure whether they actually made it to the proper North Pole.

MANY VISITORS

While visitors from many places have been part of exploring the Arctic, it's important to remember that Indigenous people have called this region home for at least 45,000 years. Scientists and historians believe that the first non-indigenous person to visit the Arctic was an Ancient Greek explorer called Pytheas, who was exploring around 300 BCE.

Snow survival
Outsiders learned how to stay warm and dry from the Inuit, making clothes out of seal and deer skin.

Expeditions travelled across the snow in **dog sleds**.

There have now been hundreds of expeditions to the North Pole. People have got there by means such as skis, planes, motorbikes, and submarines!

Teamwork
The 1909 team was made up of four Inuit – Ootah, Seegloo, Egingwah, and Ooqueah, and two men from the USA – Matthew Henson and Robert Peary.

Possible pole
A photograph was taken of the 1909 team at what they believed was the North Pole.

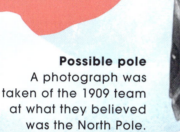

1909 expedition
Many people believe that the first non-indigenous visitors to reach the North Pole were the members of the expedition in 1909. However, evidence later emerged that the spot the team reached was a short distance from the actual North Pole.

Expeditions to the Arctic faced challenging and dangerous conditions.

LOUISE ARNER BOYD
Boyd was the first woman to fly over the North Pole in 1955, but that's not all! Over her life, she studied glaciers and new Arctic plant species. She even served as a spy during World War II.

ANTARCTIC LIFE

All the way at the bottom of the world, scientists are discovering Antarctica's secrets.

Home to the lowest temperatures ever recorded on Earth, Antarctica is not for the faint of heart. But animal life has found a way to thrive here.

Orcas and leopard seals chase penguins through the waves as the swimming birds hunt for krill. Meanwhile, albatrosses, petrels, and skuas **soar through the sky** above. Below the ice, life gets even weirder, as sponges and worms **spend their lives in total darkness**.

A humpback whale's tail breaks through the surface of the water in Antarctica.

Pack ice

Sometimes pack ice is found loose and floating freely, and other times crunched together like walls of glass shards. It is an everchanging and essential part of the Antarctic landscape.

Antarctic fur seal

Resting spot
Penguins, seals, and sea birds take a break from swimming on islands of pack ice.

Pack ice constantly **changes** and **moves.**

What is pack ice?
Pack ice is free-floating ice that's not attached to land. When small pieces of sea ice freeze together, they form drift ice. Sections of drift ice pushed together by wind or ocean currents are called ice floes. When ice floes meet and freeze together, they form vast areas of pack ice.

Rafting and ridging

When a piece of ice gets pushed up onto another, it's called rafting. Ridging is when ice gets pushed together into a solid wall.

Marching to dinner
Krill feed on the algae that grows on the underside of pack ice. This makes the ice a buffet for krill-eaters such as penguins.

Adélie penguins

Leopard seals

Feeding ground
Drawn by krill-eating penguins, leopard seals lurk in the waters below.

Pack ice changes every day, based on the temperature, wind, and flow of the ocean.

A CHANGING WORLD

Each winter, Antarctica doubles in size when the blisteringly cold water surrounding the continent freezes into thick sea ice.

Edge of pack ice in summer

SUMMER

In summer, the sea ice around Antarctica breaks up into pack ice. It then floats out to sea and melts back into the ocean.

Edge of pack ice in winter

WINTER

When winter arrives and the sunlight disappears, the surface water around Antarctica freezes once again into a thick layer of ice.

Life under the ice

Deep beneath Antarctica's surface lies a world most of us will never see. Even though no sunlight can reach it, the water below the ice shelf is rich with creatures, most of which have only recently been discovered.

Penguins

BRYOZOANS

These creatures are known as moss animals. They live on the sea floor and eat algae by filtering it out of the water.

TUBE WORMS

Just as snails produce slime, tube worms produce minerals. They form tube-like shells around their bodies for protection.

SPONGES

Did you know sponges are animals? They sit on the sea floor and filter their food from the water.

AMPHIPODS

Swarms of tiny crustaceans called amphipods have been discovered far below Antarctica's ice shelf.

Lake

DARK DEPTHS

In 2021, scientists were shocked to discover an ecosystem nearly 200 m (660 ft) below Antarctica's permanent ice sheet. It is so deep that it never sees sunlight.

Hot water
Scientists use drills and boiling water to make holes, called boreholes, through thick ice.

KRILL
See-through, shrimp-like crustaceans called krill are the foundation of the food web.

Borehole

Living on the edge
Where the ice sheet meets the sea, fish and penguins flock to eat krill. Predators such as leopard seals and orcas aren't far behind.

Leopard seal

Krill

Above water, Antarctica is considered a desert. But below, the cold waters teem with living things.

Energy source
The Sun's light energy is absorbed by plants, algae, and animals called plankton.

Keystone species

Krill gobble up tiny creatures called plankton and then are eaten themselves. This means their energy is transferred to larger animals. Without krill, the food web would fall apart.

Vital food source
Plankton are tiny plants and animals that drift with ocean currents.

Plankton

Krill

Around 6 cm (2.4 in) in length, krill are small, shrimp-like crustaceans found all over the world.
They are particularly important in Antarctica's waters, where they are at the heart of the food web – the connections between all the different species in an ecosystem.

Filter feeders

Krill use hair-like combs on their front legs to scoop up and eat plankton in the water.

Krill

Adélie penguins

Apex predator
Orcas are top-level predators with a diverse diet, including large animals such as penguins and seals.

Orca

Deep dive
Adélie penguins can swim to depths of 175 m (575 ft) to hunt down their main prey – krill.

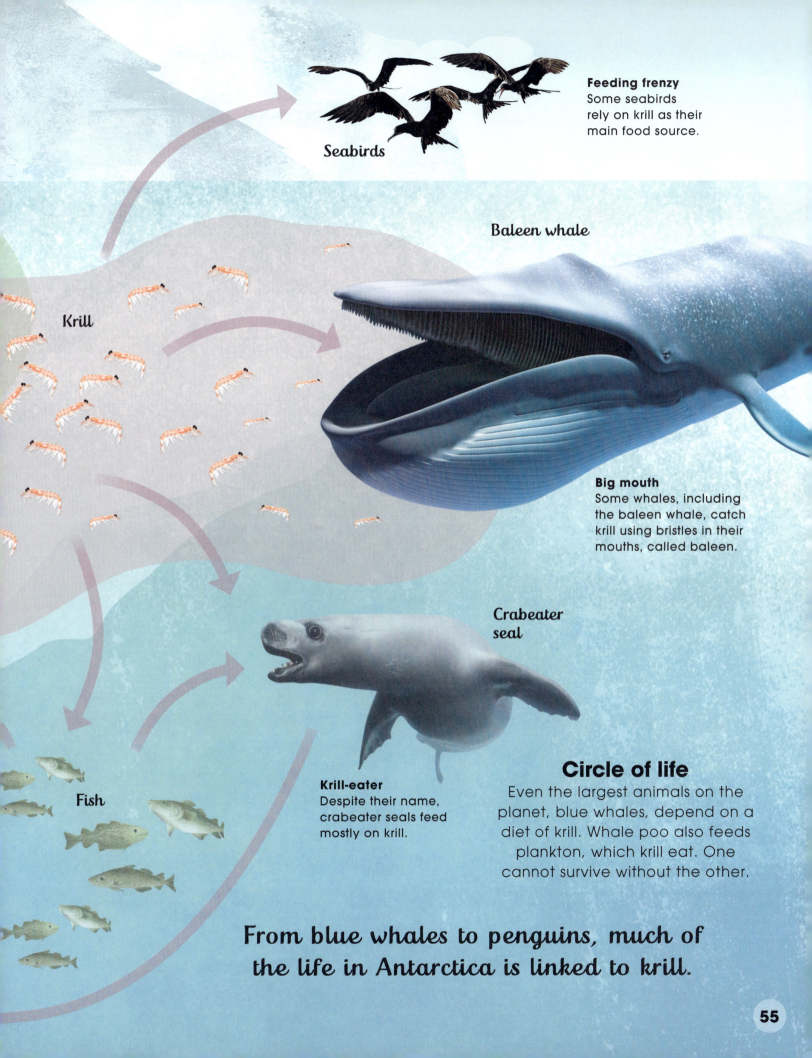

Feeding frenzy
Some seabirds rely on krill as their main food source.

Seabirds

Baleen whale

Krill

Big mouth
Some whales, including the baleen whale, catch krill using bristles in their mouths, called baleen.

Crabeater seal

Krill-eater
Despite their name, crabeater seals feed mostly on krill.

Fish

Circle of life
Even the largest animals on the planet, blue whales, depend on a diet of krill. Whale poo also feeds plankton, which krill eat. One cannot survive without the other.

From blue whales to penguins, much of the life in Antarctica is linked to krill.

Seals

Antarctica has six species of seals. They make up some of the largest predators in the region. Male elephant seals are the largest, weighing more than a pickup truck.

Elephant seal

Penguin

Eye see you
Large eyes and pupils help seals to see well in the dark gloom of the deep sea.

Fur seals

Elephant seals get their name from their trunk-like noses.

Elephant seal

Hold your breath
Elephant seals can stay underwater for nearly two hours on a single breath.

Squid

Fur seal

Pipsqueaks
Fur seals are
the smallest seals
in Antarctica.

Ross seal

Air holes
Weddell seals can
gnaw through ice to
create breathing holes.

Weddell
seal

Leopard seal

Leopards of the sea
Like their name suggests,
leopard seals are fierce
predators that prey upon
penguins, fish, squid,
and even other seals.

Penguin

Much of a seal's life
is spent under the ice, where
it's often warmer than the
world above.

Sea giants

Some of Earth's largest and most spectacular creatures call the Antarctic waters home. The cold, deep water contains lots of nutrients, and it flows up to the surface via underwater currents.

Big whale
The blue whale is the largest animal on Earth. Its heart is the size of a car.

Orca

Southern bottlenose whales

Strength in numbers
By hunting in packs, orcas can take down prey many times their size – even blue whales!

Melon-head
The bulbous forehead, known as the melon, of the southern bottlenose whale may be used for echolocation. This is when animals use sound to navigate.

TOOTHED WHALES
Toothed whales are predators. They use their sharp teeth to eat fish, squid, seabirds, and sometimes other marine mammals such as seals.

Sperm whale

Arnoux's beaked whale

Giants eating giants
Scientists believe sperm whales sometimes battle and eat giant squid in the deep ocean.

Hold your breath
The Arnoux's beaked whale can stay underwater for an hour.

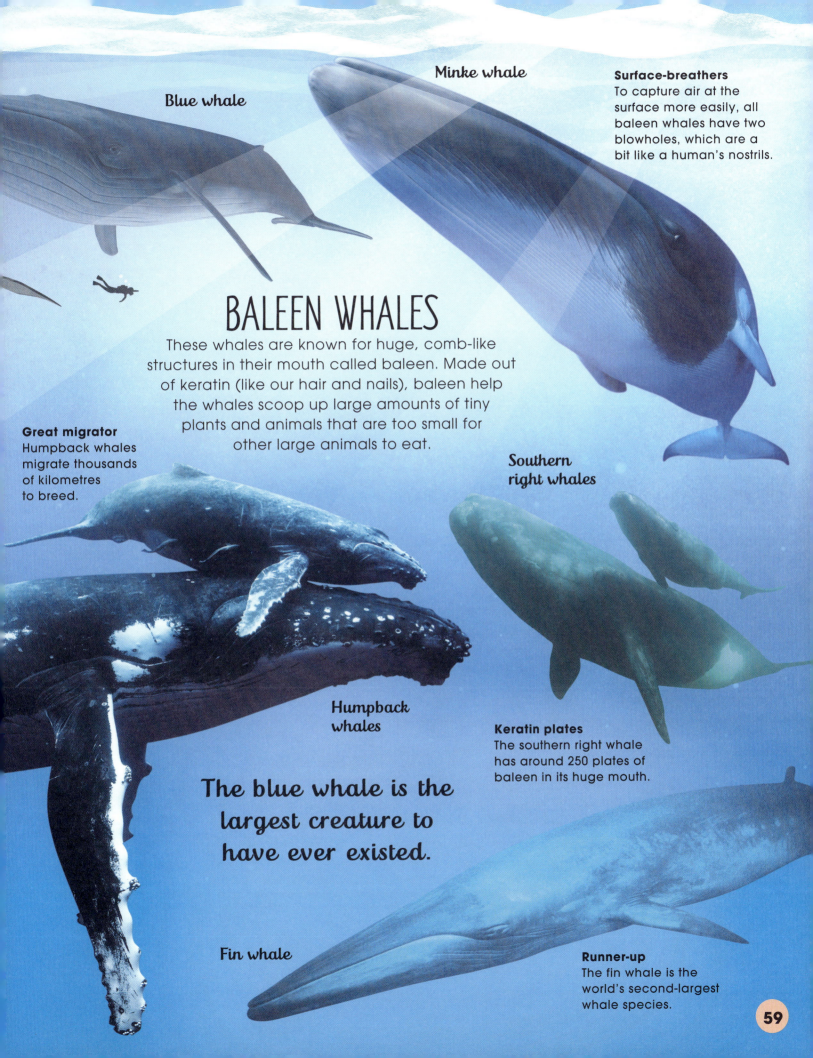

Blue whale

Minke whale

Surface-breathers
To capture air at the surface more easily, all baleen whales have two blowholes, which are a bit like a human's nostrils.

BALEEN WHALES

These whales are known for huge, comb-like structures in their mouth called baleen. Made out of keratin (like our hair and nails), baleen help the whales scoop up large amounts of tiny plants and animals that are too small for other large animals to eat.

Great migrator
Humpback whales migrate thousands of kilometres to breed.

Southern right whales

Humpback whales

Keratin plates
The southern right whale has around 250 plates of baleen in its huge mouth.

The blue whale is the largest creature to have ever existed.

Fin whale

Runner-up
The fin whale is the world's second-largest whale species.

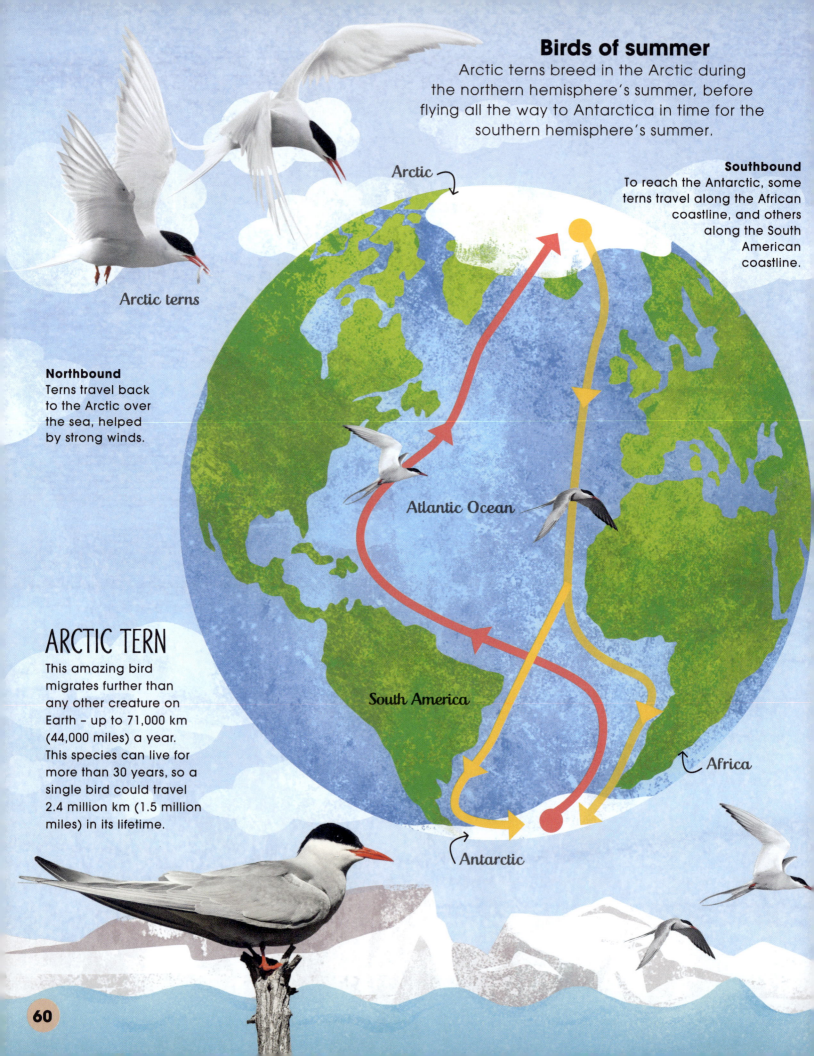

Birds of summer

Arctic terns breed in the Arctic during the northern hemisphere's summer, before flying all the way to Antarctica in time for the southern hemisphere's summer.

Arctic

Southbound
To reach the Antarctic, some terns travel along the African coastline, and others along the South American coastline.

Arctic terns

Northbound
Terns travel back to the Arctic over the sea, helped by strong winds.

Atlantic Ocean

ARCTIC TERN

This amazing bird migrates further than any other creature on Earth – up to 71,000 km (44,000 miles) a year. This species can live for more than 30 years, so a single bird could travel 2.4 million km (1.5 million miles) in its lifetime.

South America

Africa

Antarctic

GIANT PETREL

Sometimes called "stinkers" because of their love for rotting carcasses, giant petrels are also predators of penguins.

GREAT SHEARWATER

This species is one of the few birds that migrates all the way from sub-Antarctic islands to the Northern Hemisphere.

BROWN SKUA

Brown skuas spend most of their life at sea. They get much of their food by stealing it off other seabirds.

ANTARCTIC SHAG

This bird is known for its brilliant blue eyes, so it is sometimes called the blue-eyed shag.

Antarctic birds

Antarctica is famous for its penguins, but it's also home to dozens of species of amazing birds you may not have heard of before.

WANDERING ALBATROSS

These huge birds are masters of the air, staying out at sea for five to ten years before returning to land to mate.

ANTARCTIC PRION

Prions fly low over the ocean to scoop up krill and squid from the water with their beaks.

SNOWY SHEATHBILL

These pigeon-like birds scavenge for food and also eat poo. They sometimes hitchhike on passing ships.

WILSON'S STORM PETREL

This species feeds by hovering over the water like a hummingbird and snatching up small prey in its beak.

Penguins

There are 18 species of penguins across the world, but only five of these species are found on Antarctica's mainland. Penguins can't fly, but they are all excellent swimmers, thanks to powerful flippers and torpedo-shaped bodies.

Gentoo penguin

Emperor penguins

Standing tall
Weighing around 40 kg (88 lb) and measuring 115 cm (45 in) tall, the emperor penguin is the largest penguin species on Earth.

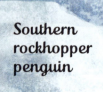

Southern rockhopper penguin

Life at sea
Macaroni penguins can spend as many as three weeks at a time out hunting in the ocean.

Island life
King penguins live and breed on islands surrounding Antarctica.

King penguin

Adaptable eyes
When we open our eyes underwater, it's blurry. But penguins are able to see well in both air and water.

Macaroni penguin

Gentoo penguins are the fastest penguins, swimming at speeds up to 35 kph (22 mph)!

Chinstrap penguin

Adélie penguin

Deep dive
Penguins spend most of their time hunting in water, sometimes diving hundreds of metres deep to catch fish, squid, and krill.

Penguins are built for swimming.

Safety in numbers
Chinstrap penguins are the most numerous penguins in the Antarctic.

63

Antarctic exploration

The South Pole is in the middle of the world's biggest, coldest, and windiest desert. However, explorers actually thought it easier to get to than the North Pole, because it is on land. The North Pole is in the middle of a frozen ocean. In the 1900s, two different expeditions set off for Antarctica, in what would become a race to the South Pole.

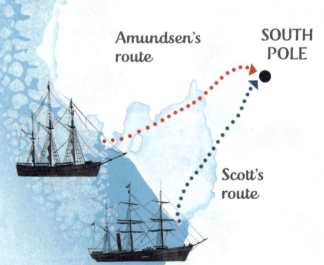

Shackleton's route

Inuit expertise
Amundsen's team survived thanks to what they learned from Inuit, such as dressing in animal skins and furs to stay warm.

Amundsen's route

SOUTH POLE

Scott's route

ROALD AMUNDSEN

On December 14, 1911, Norwegian explorer Roald Amundsen and his team became the first people to reach the South Pole. On past visits to the Arctic, they had learned ways of surviving the deadly cold from Inuit. They used dogsleds and skis to make their Antarctic journey, and all four members of the team returned safely.

There were 17 Antarctic missions from 1897 to 1922.

Shackleton's ship
The ill-fated ship was called the *Endurance*.

Against the elements
Scott's expedition faced colder weather and harsher conditions than Amundsen's.

Scullin Monolith

ROBERT SCOTT

Scott first tried and failed to reach the South Pole in 1904. He tried a second time, but when he and his team reached the South Pole on January 17, 1912, they discovered that Amundsen's team had reached it 34 days earlier. Sadly, Scott's team did not survive the journey home.

ERNEST SHACKLETON

In 1914, while trying to cross Antarctica, Shackleton's ship froze in sea ice. The team spent months on the ship, but when it sank, travelled for six days on lifeboats to Elephant Island. Shackleton then made an epic journey of nearly 1,300 km (808 miles) to find help. After 20 months, he returned every sailor safely to England.

Ship shape
Using remote-controlled submarines, scientists located the *Endurance* at the bottom of the Weddell Sea in 2022. It was still in surprisingly good shape!

INGRID CHRISTENSEN

For decades, men did not allow women to join their crews. However, in 1931, Ingrid Christensen and Mathilde Wegger became the first women to see Antarctica from a ship. Christensen returned several times, flying over the continent in 1936. In 1937, she landed at Scullin Monolith, with her three female crew members, becoming the first woman to reach the mainland.

Research stations

It takes special buildings to survive the Antarctic winter. Stilts that can be raised and lowered stop research stations from getting buried beneath snow. Each pod is used for a different purpose, from sleeping or exercise to scientific experiments.

Studying the Antarctic

In 1959, 12 nations came together to sign the Antarctic Treaty. It declared that the continent of Antarctica should only be used for peaceful purposes – that means no war, no nuclear weapons, but lots of science!

A place for science

Today, more than 50 countries have signed the Antarctic Treaty, earning Antarctica its nickname of "The International Continent".

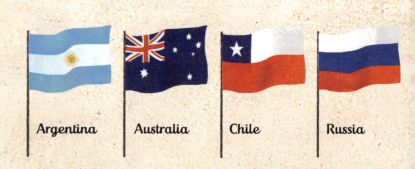

Argentina   Australia   Chile   Russia

A scientist's life

In winter, Antarctica gets so cold it hurts to breathe. Storms can last for weeks on end, and the darkness can become overwhelming. But there's also time to rock climb, ski, and even play football outside.

Antarctica has around 4,400 researchers and support staff that live there in summer, but just 1,100 people in winter.

What do they study?

A huge range of things are researched in the Antarctic, including climate change, animals, auroras, the ozone layer, and even neutrinos – tiny particles that come from space.

Gentoo penguins

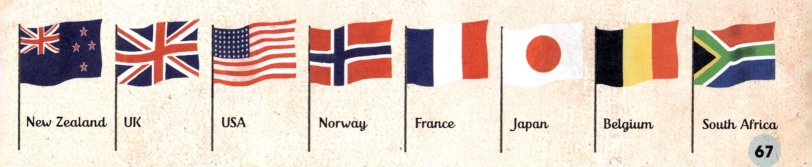

New Zealand | UK | USA | Norway | France | Japan | Belgium | South Africa

THE FROZEN WORLDS AND ME

Both the Arctic and Antarctic are threatened by the effects of climate change.

By burning fossil fuels such as coal and oil to create electricity, humans are causing Earth to grow warmer. This is already impacting the poles. As **ice sheets and glaciers melt**, ecosystems are changing faster than plants and animals can adapt. **The good news is that it's not too late to reverse these effects.**

If we work together, we can save species from extinction, restore habitats, and help people, plants, and animals to thrive. **Together, we can protect the poles.**

It's important to wrap up warm to enjoy the cold conditions of the Arctic and Antarctic.

Ice at risk

Our planet is getting warmer. By burning fossil fuels such as oil and coal and cutting down forests, humans are causing the climate to change much faster than ever before. This climate change, or global warming, is putting the poles at great risk.

The Sun warms our planet, which makes life possible, but it also gives off harmful radiation.

Melting ice

As the planet is warming up, more and more ice is melting. Polar bears, walruses, and many other creatures rely on the ice to help them get around their home. Without it, some creatures may not be able to find enough food to survive.

CLIMATE CHANGE

Earth's atmosphere acts like a greenhouse, trapping the Sun's heat and warming the Earth. But it is now locking in more heat than before.

Polar bear

Increased shipping
A rise in shipping traffic means increased pollution. It will also threaten sea animals, which could get hurt by large vessels.

Some radiation is trapped in Earth's atmosphere, causing the planet to warm up.

Some heat escapes back out into space.

Human activity causes harmful greenhouse gases to build up in the Earth's atmosphere, which trap even more of the Sun's radiation.

Rising tides
Melting ice means more water in the oceans, which causes them to rise. This puts coastal habitats everywhere at risk of flooding.

Fighting for food
Scientists worry that warmer seas could make it harder for krill to survive. This would then affect the many other animals that rely on krill for food.

Penguins

Krill

Helping the ice

Climate change is a global problem, which affects the polar regions, but also the rest of the world. We need everyone's help to fix it. There are plenty of things we can do to make the planet a cleaner, greener, and better place to live!

Bottle bird feeder

Turn it off
Not using it? Hit the switch!

Second life
Can you think of new uses for old bottles or bags?

Sort and separate
Help your adults save recyclables from the bin.

Light

Recycling

SAVE ENERGY
Most electricity comes from climate-changing fossil fuels such as coal and gas. Turning off lights and electronics when not needed helps to cut down on these fuels.

RECYCLE OR REUSE
Using things more than once or recycling them can help to cut down on the need for new materials to be made. This reduces pollution.

Even small actions that fight climate change can help save polar ice.

Go for a ride
For short trips, bikes are a great way to get around.

Bicycle helmet

WE'RE ALL IN THIS TOGETHER

Governments, businesses, and scientists can do the most to find solutions to the climate change problem. These include looking for new sources of green power, such as wind turbines and solar panels, and developing technology such as electric cars to reduce the greenhouse gases we produce.

CUT EMISSIONS

Cars powered by fossil fuels spit out harmful greenhouse gases that contribute to climate change. When you need to get around, try to walk, or take a bike, bus, or train instead.

Whale watching
Now that blue whale numbers are recovering, people can take boat trips to witness the whales in their natural habitat.

An icy success story

The blue whale is the largest animal that has ever existed – it is bigger than any of the dinosaurs. Just a few decades of hunting nearly drove these animals to extinction. When just 360 remained by the 1970s, people decided to put an end to whaling and bring blue whales back.

Now, as many as **15,000 blue whales** are alive.

There are several subspecies of blue whale, with Antarctic blue whales measuring the longest and heaviest of them all.

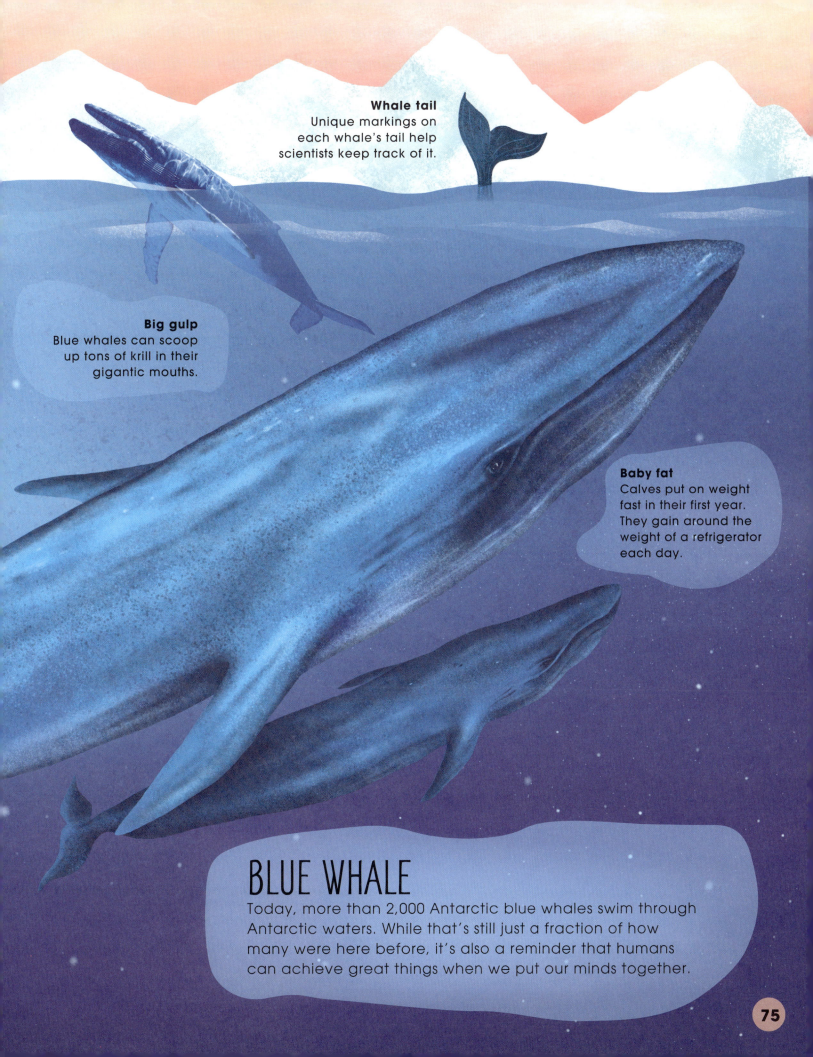

Whale tail
Unique markings on each whale's tail help scientists keep track of it.

Big gulp
Blue whales can scoop up tons of krill in their gigantic mouths.

Baby fat
Calves put on weight fast in their first year. They gain around the weight of a refrigerator each day.

BLUE WHALE

Today, more than 2,000 Antarctic blue whales swim through Antarctic waters. While that's still just a fraction of how many were here before, it's also a reminder that humans can achieve great things when we put our minds together.

Glossary

ADAPT
How a living thing changes over time to help it survive better in its environment.

ARTHROPOD
Group of invertebrates with a tough outer skeleton and a body divided into segments.

ATMOSPHERE
Thick layer of gases around Earth that protect the planet from the burning rays of the Sun.

BENTHOS
Community of living things that live on or near the seafloor.

BLOWHOLE
Nostril in the top of a whale's head that allows it to breathe.

CARNIVORE
Animal that eats other animals.

CLIMATE CHANGE
Change in temperature and weather across the Earth. It could be natural or caused by human activity, such as pollution.

CRUSTACEAN
Type of arthropod which is usually aquatic and breathes through gills, such as lobsters and shrimp.

DAM
Barrier that holds back water.

ECHOLOCATION
A process some animals use to locate objects with sound rather than sight. They produce sound waves and listen to how long it takes the sound to echo back to them. This helps them communicate or find where prey is located.

ECOSYSTEM
Community of living things and their environment – including the soil, water, and air around them.

EVOLVE
The way living things change and adapt over time to help them survive.

FATTY TISSUE
Type of body tissue where fat is stored.

FOSSIL FUELS
Fuels made from animals and plants that died millions of years ago, such as coal and oil.

GREENHOUSE GASES
Gases in the Earth's atmosphere that trap heat and warm the planet.

HEMISPHERE
Top or bottom half of Earth. The Arctic is in the northern hemisphere, and Antarctica is in the southern hemisphere.

INDIGENOUS PEOPLE
Peoples who are or are related to the earliest known inhabitants of a place.

INUK
Person belonging to the Inuit group of peoples.

INVERTEBRATE
Animal without a backbone.

KEYSTONE SPECIES

Living thing that helps to hold its habitat together.

LANDMASS

Continent or large area of land.

LARVA

Insect after it hatches from an egg, but before the adult stage.

MAGNETIC FIELD

Area of magnetism surrounding a magnet or a planet, star, or galaxy.

MIGRATE

Move from one region to another.

MINERAL

A group of chemicals forming a solid that occurs in nature, such as crystals.

NOMADIC

Not living in one fixed place, but rather moving around an area in search of food and water.

ORBIT

Path an object takes around another due to gravity, such as how planets travel around the Sun.

PARASITE

Animal that lives on and feeds off another animal.

PERMAFROST

A layer of permanently frozen soil underground.

POLAR

To do with the areas near the North and South Poles.

PREDATOR

Animal that hunts other animals for food.

PREY

Animal that is hunted for food by other animals.

REMOTE

Far away from busy areas.

SCAVENGER

Animal that feeds on the remains of dead animals.

SOLAR WIND

Stream of charged particles from the Sun.

THAW

Melt.

TORPEDO

Thin, cylinder-shaped weapon fired from a submarine.

TUSK

Long tooth that grows from the jaws of animals, such as elephants and narwhals. Sometimes called ivory, it can be carved easily and used to make jewellery.

VERTEBRATE

Animal with a backbone.

WHALING

Hunting whales for their meat and blubber.

Index

Acknowledgements

The publisher would like to thank the following people for their assistance:
Susie Rae for the index and proofreading.

PICTURE CREDITS

The publisher would like to thank the following for their kind permission to reproduce their photographs: (Key: a-above; b-below/bottom; c-centre; f-far; l-left; r-right; t-top)

1 123RF.com: Eric Isselee / isselee (bl). **Dreamstime.com:** Agami Photo Agency (c); Isselee (cr); Deaddogdodge (cra); Sergey Uryadnikov / Surz01 (clb). **4-5 Dreamstime.com:** Oskari Porkka. **5-73 Dreamstime.com:** Designprintck (Background). **6-7 Dreamstime.com:** Ruslan Nassyrov / Ruslanchik. **6 Dorling Kindersley:** Andrew Beckett (tr); Tracy Morgan (c). **Dreamstime.com:** Deaddogdodge (crb); Luis Leamus (tc); Helen Panphilova / Gazprom (cra); Konstantin Pukhov / Kostya6969 (cl). **naturepl.com:** Eric Baccega (cra). **7 Alamy Stock Photo:** Keren Su / China Span (cl); Ray Wilson (tr); Roger Clark (cb); H. Mark Weidman Photography (cr); Zoonar / Dmytro Pylypenko (crb). **Dorling Kindersley:** leksele (tl). **Dreamstime.com:** Jan Martin Will (tc/Penguin). **naturepl.com:** Colin Monteath (cb/grass); Tui De Roy (cla). **Shutterstock.com:** David Osborn (clb); Tarpan (cb/seal). **8-9 Dreamstime.com:** Hramovnick (t/icicles); Prachenko Iryna (t); Christopher Wood (ca); Robkna (cb). **8 Dreamstime.com:** Steve Allen (br); Alexey Sedov (cl); Rgbe (cl); Luis Leamus (bl). **9 Dreamstime.com:** Deaddogdodge (ca); Alexey Sedov (cra); Fotokon (c); Photographerlondon (clb); Ndp (bc, crb). **10 Dreamstime.com:** Scattoselvaggio (crb). **Getty Images:** Moment / Javier Fernndez Snchez (clb). **11 Alamy Stock Photo:** blickwinkel / AGAMI / A. Ghignone (clb). **Getty Images:** DmitryND (crb). **12 123RF.com:** Steve Byland / steve_byland (cla). **Alamy Stock Photo:** All Canada Photos / Ron Erwin (crb). **Dreamstime.com:** Perchhead (cra). **Getty Images / iStock:** E+ / Oleh_Slobodeniuk (clb). **13 Dreamstime.com:** Iakov Filimonov / Jackf (crb). **Getty Images:** Steve Austin (clb). **14 Alamy Stock Photo:** imageBROKER / Michael Weberberger (clb/whale). **Dorling Kindersley:** Andrew Beckett (tr). **Dreamstime.com:** Iakov Filimonov / Jackf (cb); Sergey Korotkov (clb). **naturepl.com:** Tui De Roy (ca). **16-17 naturepl.com:** Norbert Wu. **16 naturepl.com:** Jordi Chias (cra). **17 naturepl.com:** Norbert Wu (cra). **18 Dreamstime.com:** Christopher Ewing (ca). **19 Dreamstime.com:** Gail Johnson (br); Wirestock (bl). **20-21 Alamy Stock Photo:** Ashley Cooper pics. **20 Alamy Stock Photo:** Ashley Cooper pics (br). **24-25 Alamy Stock Photo:** robertharding / David Jenkins. **26 Alamy Stock Photo:** Arterra Picture Library / Arndt Sven-Erik (br); Ken Archer / DanitaDelimont (cla); Tom Ingram (bc). **Dreamstime.com:** Agami Photo Agency (c/x4); Lee Amery (fr); Andreanita (cr, c); Akinshin (clb). **27 Alamy Stock Photo:** All Canada Photos / Benjamin Dy (cr); blickwinkel / McPHOTO / TRU (clb); Arterra Picture Library / van der Meer Marica (crb, bl); Arterra Picture Library / Arndt Sven-Erik (fcra, br). **Dreamstime.com:** Erectus (cl, cra); Vladimir Melnikov (ca); Koldunova (c); Lillian Tveit (cb). **28 Dreamstime.com:** Jim Cumming (b); Mikelane45 (cra); Marcin Wojciechowski (cl). **Shutterstock.com:** Jukka Jantunen. **29 Dreamstime.com:** Per Bjorkdahl (ca); Samsem67 (tl); Mikhail Blajenov (tc); Denis Pepin (bl); Sergey Uryadnikov / Surz01 (cla); Lanaufoto (c). **30 123RF.com:** Vasiliy Vishnevskiy / ornitolog82 (tl). **Dorling Kindersley:** Roger Tidman (c). **Dreamstime.com:** Agami Photo Agency (tc); Lee Amery (cl); Wkruck (tl/Red-throated diver); Jeff Grabert (cja); Paul Reeves (ca); Frank Fichtmueller (bl); Vladimir Melnik (bc); Dinozzaver (br). **Getty Images:** Daniel Parent (tr). **30-31 Dreamstime.com:** Neil Burton (b). **31 Dorling Kindersley:** Chris Gomersall Photography (bl); Mike Lane (ca); Windrush

Photos (c). **Dreamstime.com:** Agami Photo Agency (br); Razvan Zinica (tl); Brian Kushner / Bkushner (cla); Andreanita (cl); Julian Popov (ca/gannets); Henkqbeaard (cra); Smitty411 (cb/Sanderling); David Spates (crb); Mogens Trolle (crb/Northern fulmar). **32 Dreamstime.com:** Planetfelicity (cr, b). **33 Alamy Stock Photo:** Franco Banfi / Nature Picture Library (bl); SCOTLAND: The Big Picture / Nature Picture Library (cr). **Dreamstime.com:** Doug Allan (ca); Kevin Schafer (cra). **naturepl.com:** Chris Gomersall (crb); Tony Wu (tl); Pal Hermansen (tr). **34-35 Dreamstime.com:** Planetfelicity. **36 Alamy Stock Photo:** John Delapp / Alaska Stock / Design Pics Inc (tl); Louise Murray (c). **Dreamstime.com:** Bborriss (cl); Anna Markova (fclb); Kateryna Mashkevych (clb); Vitaserendipity (bl); Digitalimagined (cb); MikeModular (br). **36-37 Alamy Stock Photo:** GenOne360 (cb). **37 Alamy Stock Photo:** blickwinkel / McPHOTO / BRS (cl); GM Photo Images (ca); Guy Edwardes / Nature Picture Library (tr). **Dreamstime.com:** Jay Beiler (tl); Tony Campbell (cla); Lars Ove Jonsson (tr); Ordinka26 (ca/yellow Saxifraga); Tanchic (bl); Olya Solodenko (br). **38 123RF.com:** Charles Brutlag (clb). **Alamy Stock Photo:** Phil Savoie / Nature Picture Library (cb). **naturepl.com:** Bryan and Cherry Alexander (cr); Jenny E. Ross (cl). **39 Alamy Stock Photo:** Daniel Heuclin / Nature Picture Library (c/Human botfly). **Dreamstime.com:** Risto Hunt (cb); Orionmystery (c). **naturepl.com:** Nick Upton (br). **40 Alamy Stock Photo:** Cindy Hopkins (br). **Dreamstime.com:** Alexander Khitrov. **42 Alamy Stock Photo:** Frans Lemmens (c). **Dreamstime.com:** Vladimir Konjushenko (br). **42-43 Dreamstime.com:** Checco (clb). **43 Dreamstime.com:** Hel080808 (tl). **44-45 Alamy Stock Photo:** Richard Ryland. **44 Dreamstime.com:** Ruslan Gilmanshin (crb). **47 Alamy Stock Photo:** Historic Collection (bc); Tango Images (cra). **48-49 Dreamstime.com:** Slew11. **50 Dorling Kindersley:** Alan Burger (c). **Dreamstime.com:** Agami Photo Agency (tc). **51 Alamy Stock Photo:** Helmut Cornell (clb). **Dreamstime.com:** Jonathan R. Green / Jonagreen (cla); Jan Martin Will (ca). **52 Dreamstime.com:** Vladislav Jirousek (cra). **53 Alamy Stock Photo:** Michael Nolan / robertharding (ca/leopard seal). **Dreamstime.com:** Vladislav Jirousek (ca); Robertlasalle (cra). **54-55 123RF.com:** Eugene Sergeev. **Dorling Kindersley:** Natural History Museum, London (c). **54 Alamy Stock** Photo: Fred Olivier / Nature Picture Library (fcrb). **Dreamstime.com:** Allexxandar (c); Simone Gatterwe / Smgirly (bl); Sandra Nelson (clb). **55 Dreamstime.com:** Leonello Calvetti (cra). **naturepl.com:** Jordi Chias (cb); Doug Perrine (tc). **56 Alamy Stock Photo:** imageBROKER / Jurgen & Christine Sohns (clb). **Getty Images:** by wildestanimal (cr); Peter Giovannini (cla). **naturepl.com:** Jordi Chias (cl). **57 Alamy Stock Photo:** Alasdair Turner / Cavan Images (cla); Norbert Wu / Minden Pictures (cl). **Dreamstime.com:** Staphy (ca). **naturepl.com:** Jordi Chias (cr). **58 Alamy Stock Photo:** Blue Planet Archive FBA (bl); Andreas Maecker (cla). **Dreamstime.com:** Simone Gatterwe / Smgirly (cra). **naturepl.com:** Richard Herrmann (c). **58-59 Alamy Stock** Photo: George Karbus Photography / Cultura Creative RF (cb). **59 Alamy Stock Photo:** Jurgen Freund / Nature Picture Library (tr); Wildestanimal (cr); Doc White / Nature Picture Library (br). **Getty Images / iStock:** bbevren (tl). **60 Alamy Stock Photo:** Marie Read / Nature Picture Library (tr). **Dreamstime.com:** Hakoar (cla, c, br, crb); Pisotckii (bl). **61 Alamy Stock Photo:** Luis Quinta / Nature Picture Library (tc); Chris & Monique Fallows / Nature Picture Library (cr); Markus Varesvuo / Nature Picture Library (crb). **Dreamstime.com:** Agami Photo Agency (clb); Ondej Prosick (tl); Tarpan (br). **naturepl.com:** Claudio Contreras (cb); Brent Stephenson (tr). **62 Dreamstime.com:** Andybignellphoto (crb, tr); Gentoomultimedia (cl). **63 Alamy Stock Photo:** Zoonar / Sergey Korotkov (cla). **Dreamstime.com:** Isselee (tc); Willtu (clb); Angela Perryman (cr). **Getty Images:** Andrew Peacock (bc). **64 Getty Images:** Bettmann

(clb). **65 Dreamstime.com:** Gentoomultimedia (cl). **Getty Images:** Bettmann (tr); Hulton-Deutsch Collection / Corbis (cl). **67 Getty Images:** Andrew Peacock (crb). **68-69 Dreamstime.com:** Polina Bublik. **70 Dreamstime.com:** Yan Keung Lee (t); Ondej Prosick (clb). **71 Dreamstime.com:** Silvae1 (br); Tarpan (bl, fbl, bc). **72 Dreamstime.com:** Airborne77 (cr); Rawin Tanpin (bl); Lianna2013 (cl); Tatiana Kuklina (tr). **73 Dreamstime.com:** Cretolamna (c). **74 naturepl.com:** Doug Perrine (tr). **75 Getty Images:** SCIEPRO / Science Photo Library (tl)

Cover images: *Front:* **123RF.com:** Eric Isselee / isselee cl; **Dreamstime.com:** Luis Leamus tl, Sergey Uryadnikov / Surz01 cra, Vladimir Seliverstov / Vladsilver crb; *Back:* **123RF.com:** Eric Isselee / isselee cr; **Dreamstime.com:** Luis Leamus cla, Vladimir Seliverstov / Vladsilver clb; *Spine:* **Dreamstime.com:** Sergey Uryadnikov / Surz01 t

All other images © Dorling Kindersley

ABOUT THE ILLUSTRATOR

Claire McElfatrick is a freelance artist. Her beautiful hand-drawn and collaged illustrations are inspired by her home in rural England. Claire has illustrated all the other books in this series: *The Magic and Mystery of Trees*, *The Book of Brilliant Bugs*, *Earth's Incredible Oceans*, and *The Extraordinary World of Birds*.